Machine Poems

Compiled by John Foster

Contents
In the kitchen   *Tony Bradman*   2
The runaway vacuum cleaner   *Tony Bradman*   4
I've made a machine   *Richard James*   8
The diggers   *Marian Swinger*   10
The time machine   *Richard James*   12
I tried to play a tape   *John Foster*   15
The computer   *John Coldwell*   16

Acknowledgements
The Editor and Publisher wish to thank the following who have kindly given permission for the use of copyright material:
Tony Bradman for 'In the kitchen' and 'The runaway vacuum cleaner' both © 1996 Tony Bradman; John Coldwell for 'The computer' © 1996 John Coldwell; John Foster for 'I tried to play a tape' © 1996 John Foster; Richard James for 'I've made a machine' and 'The time machine' both © 1996 Richard James; Marian Swinger for 'The diggers' © 1996 Marian Swinger.

In the kitchen

The dishwasher's sloshing,
The boiler is humming,
The washing machine's in a spin;
The toaster is popping,
The cat flap is banging,
The cat's trying hard to get in.

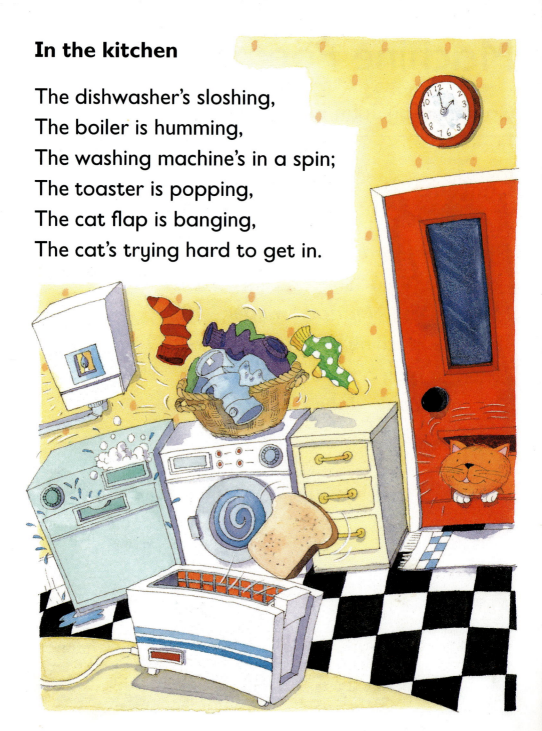

The radio's crackling,
The microwave's pinging,
The kettle is blowing its spout;
But worse than all this,
Our dad's started singing!
Now the cat's trying hard to get out!

Tony Bradman

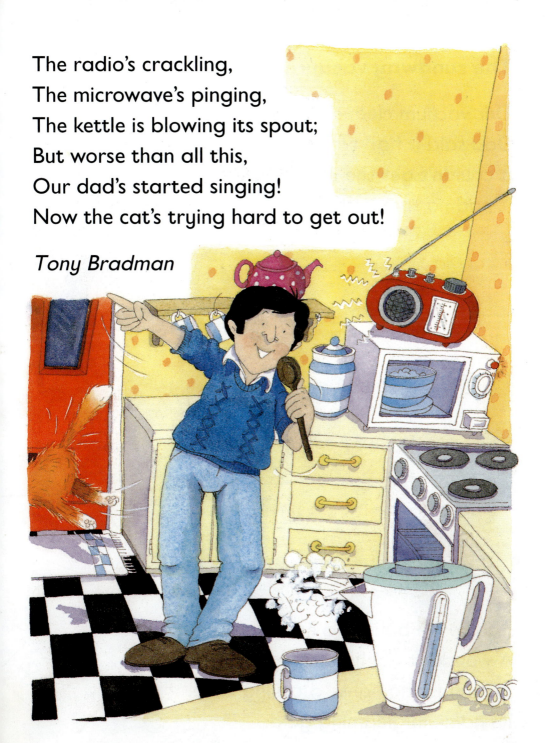

The runaway vacuum cleaner

Our vacuum cleaner was worn out,
Dad said it had to go;
It couldn't get the carpets clean,
It had no suck, just blow.

And so we bought a new machine,
A wonder to behold;
With flashing lights, a coiling tube,
Its name in gleaming gold.

Dad pressed the switch, the vacuum jumped,
There was a mighty roar,
It dragged Dad all around the room,
Then pulled him through the door.

It flew around the kitchen,
Then caught us unawares,
By flying round and round the hall
And shooting up the stairs.

We heard a crash! and tinkle!
The vacuum had escaped!
It smashed right through a window
(We hope Dad wasn't scraped!)

A week went by and then we got
A postcard from our dad.
It said he was in Egypt,
And that things weren't too bad.

'The vacuum cleaner's happy,' it said,
'It thinks this place is grand.
We'll see you in a year or two
When we've cleaned up all this sand!'

Tony Bradman

I've made a machine

I've made a machine
That can fly, drive and float.
It's got wings like a plane
And sails like a boat.
It can rocket through space.
It can dive in the sea.
It can dig through the ground.
It can climb up a tree.
I've made a machine.
It's fast and it's smart –
If only I knew
How to get it to start!

Richard James

The diggers

The diggers grab the soil up
in their mighty metal jaws.
They growl around the roadworks
like a herd of dinosaurs.
They look so much like monsters
with their rows of metal teeth,
tossing, digging, chomping
at the earth and rocks beneath.
They crunch and chew all day.
Their mighty engines roar.
They prowl around the roadworks
like a herd of dinosaurs.

Marian Swinger

The time machine

Roll up, roll up, and on you climb,
I'll take you travelling back through time.
I'll show you things you've never seen.
All aboard my time machine!

Count down from ten. We're off so fast
That years and years are whizzing past.
We've stopped. Where are we? In a wood.
A man in green: it's Robin Hood!

And off again through history,
Let's stop in forty-five BC.
Look! Romans marching to and fro.
They don't look friendly. Time to go.

And further back and further back
We land now on a forest track.
No human footprints on the ground.
No people yet, so what's that sound?

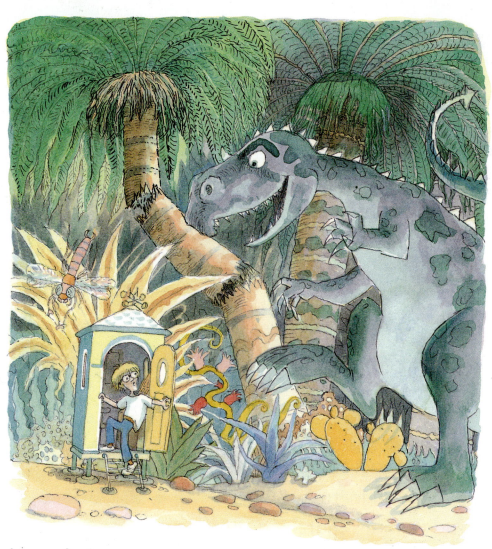

A crash, a grunt, a groan, a roar —
Look out! A long lost dinosaur!
Quick, back on board, count down from ten —
Phew! Just in time, we're home again.

Richard James

I tried to play a tape

I tried to play a tape
in the video today.
I pressed it to rewind,
then I pressed it to play.

But instead of pictures
on the screen, all that I got
were fuzzy lines as twisted tape
got tangled in the slot!

John Foster

The computer

Samantha Bean,
Samantha Bean,
Sat far too close
To the computer screen.

While she was playing
'Sonic Death Ride',
A hand leapt out
And dragged her inside.

John Coldwell